THE FUNERAL ARRANGEMENT
CHOICE GUIDE

The Funeral Arrangement Choice Guide

*Helping You Cope with
a Loved One's Death*

DALLAS ALLEN POLEN, JR.

Servant Publications
Ann Arbor, Michigan

Vine Books is an imprint of Servant Publications especially designed to serve evangelical Christians.

Published by Servant Publications
P.O. Box 8617
Ann Arbor, Michigan 48107

Biblical quotations are from the New Revised Standard Version of the Bible, © 1989 by the Division of Christian Education of the National Council of Churches of Christ in the United States of America. Used by permission. All rights reserved.

96 97 98 99 00 10 9 8 7 6 5 4 3 2 1

Printed in the United States of America
ISBN 0-89283-969-4

LIBRARY OF CONGRESS CATALOGING-IN-PUBLICATION DATA

Polen, Dallas Allen.
    The funeral arrangement choice guide : helping you cope with a loved one's death / Dallas Allen Polen, Jr.
        p.   cm.
    ISBN 0-89283-969-4
    1. Death—Social aspects—United States.   2. Funeral rites and cere-
monies—United States—Planning.   3. Bereavement—United States—
Psychological aspects.   I. Title.
HQ1073.5.U6P65 1996
306.88—dc20
                                                                95-52896
                                                                    CIP

But those who wait for the Lord
   shall renew their strength,
they shall mount up with wings like
   eagles,
they shall run and not be weary,
they shall walk and not faint.

ISAIAH 40:31

Dedication

As an expression of appreciation and gratitude, *The Funeral Arrangement Choice Guide* (hereafter, *The Choice Guide*) is dedicated to the people who shared their experiences in order that it might be written. Their experiences are reflected in the recommendations and suggestions of *The Choice Guide*. I have special admiration for their willingness to remember and recall their pain—to relive some of it—that this volume might be available to help you.

Thank you to... Eula Boylan, John Boylan, Kent Carmichael, Emmalie Cowherd, June Meyers Cunningham, Aileen DeBruce, Archie DeBruce, Indus Dey, Charolette Elliot, Lynda Fort, Gretchen Gee, Wanda Luna, Irene Morris, Jim Myers, Larry Rumburg, Lindy Rumburg, Greg Soelter, James "Jay" Stewart, Ethel Stotts, Pat Traster, Madison Traster, Ethel Turner.

In its strengths and usefulness, *The Choice Guide* is much more *their* book than my book, although I take full responsibility for the weaknesses and failures it may contain.

CONTENTS

Acknowledgments

Thank you to my wife, Joyce, without whose encouragement, help, and supportive presence I never would have begun this project, let alone finished it.

Thank you to my doctors of ministry project advisors, Dr. Kyle Maxwell and Dr. Roy Steinhoff Smith, at Phillips Theological Seminary in Enid and Tulsa, Oklahoma. I am especially grateful for Roy, who, as the primary advisor, not only was an appropriately demanding taskmaster but also an authentic friend.

Thank you to Jim Spooner, whose technical computer knowledge and skills have kept my computer operative and helped me better utilize its capabilities.

D. Allen Polen, Jr.
Hutchinson, Kansas
All Saints' Day, 1995

I lift up my eyes to the hills—
  from where will my help come?
My help comes from the Lord,
  who made heaven and earth.

PSALM 121:1-2

What Is *The Choice Guide?*
How and Why Was It Written?

The Choice Guide is an excellent resource for pastors or others (family, friends, church, support groups, Sunday School classes) to give to primary survivors at the time of a death. This guide provides the bereaved with step-by-step guidance about the decisions they must make and the choices they have. It was originally planned and designed for this purpose.

The Choice Guide can also serve as a preplanner you can use to provide for your survivors: (1) facts they will need, and (2) information about your choices and preferences at the time of your death. It will help them know what decisions they must make and what choices they have.

HOW WAS THE CHOICE GUIDE WRITTEN?

The Choice Guide was written within the context of a United Methodist church where I served as pastor. It is based on the actual experience of two dozen primary survivors. On every page, *The Choice Guide* provides what they said would have been helpful to them when they had primary responsibility for making arrangements following a death.

The quotations found throughout the book, unless otherwise noted, are statements from the two dozen people who shared their experiences in order to make this book possible. These quotations reflect what they learned and what they suggest for others.

The information will be useful to almost anyone, although Christians from other traditions may notice a United Methodist flavor of the book. Those who shared their experiences for this book were mostly United Methodist. Also included was a person from the Church of God (Anderson, Indiana) tradition and a member of the Disciples of Christ.

WHY WAS THE CHOICE GUIDE WRITTEN?

For many, probably most, North American families, one of the three largest consumer purchases of a lifetime—the other two are automobiles and homes—is the combination of goods and services needed for arrangements when death occurs. Because funeral arrangements and merchandise are so expensive, we need guidance from sources besides funeral industry professionals.

Survivors have choices. There are, in fact, many options. Survivors need to know what options are possible.

Primary survivors are in *shock* when death occurs. Their minds may not work well. They may never have faced such a situation before. They need help: clear, orderly, easily used, well planned, step-by-step help. This guide has been designed to provide that help.

When we are in shock, the temptation is to let others "take care of us." However, making choices is psychologically and spiritually healing. Grief and recovery from loss by death take time—from eighteen months to three or four years. This healing begins best when survivors actively participate and make choices as arrangements are made.

Several people commented about the length of *The Choice Guide.* The length reflects the large number of decisions that must be made—which is another reason *The Choice Guide* was written.

> *And Jesus came and said to them,*
> *"… And remember, I am with*
> *you always.…"*
>
> MATTHEW 28:18A, 20B

Where can I go from your spirit?
Or where can I flee from your presence?
If I ascend to heaven, you are there;
if I make my bed in Sheol, you are there.
If I take the wings of the morning
and settle at the farthest limits of the sea,
even there your hand shall lead me,
and your right hand shall hold me fast.
If I say, "Surely the darkness shall cover me,
and the light around me become night,"
even the darkness is not dark to you;
the night is as bright as the day,
for darkness is as light to you.

PSALM 139:7-12

How to Use *The Choice Guide*

1. Quickly scan the *Contents* (page 9) and the *checklists* (at the ends of three primary sections of the book) to get a general feeling for what you will need to think about, decide, and do. This book is divided into four primary sections: (1) Day of the Death, (2) Day after the Death, (3) Choices for the Service, and (4) Getting Help Afterward.

2. Thumb through *The Choice Guide,* noting particularly the *workbook pages* where you will need to write information.

3. Note the "To Do Later" List, the Blank Pages for Notes, and the Appointment Schedule at the very back of *The Choice Guide.*

4. Do write in *The Choice Guide.* It is designed to be a *workbook.* Keep notes, lists, and appointments in it— all in one place.

Remember: *The Choice Guide* is not meant to be followed rigidly. It is intended to guide your choosing, not tell you exactly what to do. Your unique circumstances probably will make it necessary to vary from what is suggested.

The emphasis is on *choice:* This book will help you realize that you have choices, to discover the choices you have, and to encourage you to make choices. Some suggestions in *The Choice Guide* may feel inappropriate to you—and may surprise or shock you. For someone else they may be appropriate. It is a matter of choice.

For I am convinced that neither death, nor life,... nor things present, nor things to come,... nor anything else in all creation, will be able to separate us from the love of God in Christ Jesus our Lord.

Romans 8:38-39

As Christians, solidly rooted in Scripture and powerfully grounded in the resurrection faith, we choose to trust faithfully that *God is with us always*—in sorrow as well as joy—and that nothing, not even death, can take God's love away. In your pain and sorrow, remember always: The Lord is with you!

Note to pastors and funeral directors:
If you give *The Choice Guide* to survivors at the time of death, it is suggested that you take a few minutes to "walk" through it with them and help them become familiar with the contents.

The Lord is my shepherd, I shall not want.
   He makes me lie down in green pastures;
he leads me beside still waters;
   he restores my soul.
He leads me in right paths
   for his name's sake.
Even though I walk through the darkest valley,
   I fear no evil;
for you are with me;
   your rod and your staff—
   they comfort me.

PSALM 23:1-4

The Day of the Death

DO NOT HURRY

Take the time you need to make the choices you must make. You do not have to hurry. These are important choices. Later, you will feel best about your choices if you make them carefully, thoughtfully, prayerfully—and without rushing.

YOU ARE IN SHOCK

You may feel that you *can't think* and that your mind is "kind of numb." Your common sense may not be at its best. You probably will do what you have to do automatically, hardly present in mind, functioning on "automatic pilot." You may have trouble remembering what to do next. Later you may not remember much of what happens in the next few days.

You may not *eat or sleep normally*. You may feel *scared*. These are the normal effects of shock. *It is okay for you to be this way.* Your feelings are normal.

CHOOSE A TRUSTED CONSULTANT-FRIEND

Because of shock, you are "not yourself," even if you think you are. Many people find it helpful to choose someone from among friends or family who is able to be a consultant or confidant through these difficult days.

This person is someone who right now is more able than you to think clearly.

This is someone with whom you may talk, check things out, discuss choices, and clarify your feelings and perceptions.

This may be a person who has been through a similar experience and "knows the ropes."

POSSIBLE PEOPLE FOR
"TRUSTED CONSULTANT-FRIEND":

_____ Phone_____

_____ Phone_____

_____ Phone_____

CALL YOUR PASTOR AS SOON AS POSSIBLE

Ask a nurse, your doctor, a neighbor, or friend to call your pastor. *Where can this person tell your pastor you will be?* At the hospital? At home? Some other place?

See page 41 for what you will need to know for your first meeting with your pastor.

YOUR PASTOR'S PHONE NUMBERS:

Pastor's Name _____

Church _____

Home _____

BEGIN A "TO DO LATER" LIST

Many things will come to mind that you will need to do after the services are completed. Jot them down the end of this book so you will remember them. The pages have been prepared especially for this purpose.

WHOM TO NOTIFY FIRST

The "first round" of notifications should be telephoning people whose traveling arrangements and work schedules will affect the choice of the time for the services. One of your helpers could make these phone calls for you, if you do not feel able to do so.

- Ask them to indicate, in their best judgment, when they can arrive.

- Tell them that you will call them back once the service times have been chosen.

List below the names and phone numbers of those who need to be notified first:

_____ Phone_____

_____ Phone_____

_____ Phone_____

_____ Phone_____

_____ Phone_____

_____ Phone_____

OTHERS TO BE NOTIFIED

What people—among both family and friends—do you want to be sure are personally notified *before they read about the death in a newspaper.* Do these things to double-check your list-making:

- Did the person leave a prepared list of people to notify? Check *personal papers.*

- Can you locate a *family address book* or a *Christmas card list?*

- As you make or check the notification list, remember to consider the following categories of people:

  Family—emotionally close

  Friends that care—recent

  Family—emotionally more distant

  Friends that care—past

  Work associates of the deceased

  Work associates of primary survivors

The following pages are worksheets to help you build a list of people to notify.

FAMILY

EMOTIONALLY CLOSE

Name	Phone No.	Contacted
_____	_____	_____
_____	_____	_____
_____	_____	_____
_____	_____	_____
_____	_____	_____
_____	_____	_____
_____	_____	_____
_____	_____	_____
_____	_____	_____
_____	_____	_____
_____	_____	_____
_____	_____	_____
_____	_____	_____

FRIENDS THAT CARE

RECENT

Name	Phone No.	Contacted

FAMILY

EMOTIONALLY MORE DISTANT

Name	Phone No.	Contacted

FRIENDS THAT CARE
PAST

Name	Phone No.	Contacted
_____	_____	_____
_____	_____	_____
_____	_____	_____
_____	_____	_____
_____	_____	_____
_____	_____	_____
_____	_____	_____
_____	_____	_____
_____	_____	_____
_____	_____	_____
_____	_____	_____
_____	_____	_____
_____	_____	_____
_____	_____	_____
_____	_____	_____
_____	_____	_____

WORK ASSOCIATES

OF THE DECEASED

Name	Phone No.	Contacted
_____	_____	_____
_____	_____	_____
_____	_____	_____
_____	_____	_____
_____	_____	_____
_____	_____	_____
_____	_____	_____
_____	_____	_____
_____	_____	_____
_____	_____	_____
_____	_____	_____
_____	_____	_____
_____	_____	_____
_____	_____	_____

WORK ASSOCIATES

OF PRIMARY SURVIVORS

Name	Phone No.	Contacted

LET OTHERS HELP

Friends and family members may ask what they can do to help you. If they ask, let them help! Here are some examples of the many "little things" which are important but will be difficult for you to get done. You could ask someone to:

• Keep a list of food gifts brought to your home. The list needs to include what the food is, who brought it, and if a dish needs to be returned.

• Purchase an inexpensive guest book for you to have at home to keep a record of the people who visit.

• Make some of the notification telephone calls.

• Answer your phone and take messages. It may be helpful to keep a written record of telephone calls. A friend—or a series of friends—may be able to do this.

• Answer the door when people come to visit.

• Be "someone at the house" when you must be gone. This person can answer the telephone and the door, take messages, and provide security by his or her presence.

• Get dry cleaning done, if needed. Clothing for the deceased or for you to wear to the services may need dry cleaning. A friend or family member could take and pick up this cleaning.

- Cancel appointments or meetings for yourself, other family members, or the deceased. A friend or other family member can make telephone notifications of your need to cancel. This includes things like appointments for doctors, dentists, haircuts, etc.

Other things friends and family can do to help:

_____

_____

_____

_____

_____

For it was you who formed my inward parts;
you knit me together in my mother's womb.
I praise you, for I am fearfully and
wonderfully made.

PSALM 139:13-14A

CHOOSE A FUNERAL DIRECTOR

A funeral director's purpose is to coordinate arrangements and to provide services and merchandise needed or chosen to care for the body.

When you choose a funeral director, three practical considerations are important guides for your choice:

First is preference: Did the person who died ever express an opinion or preference about a funeral home?

Second is reputation: Are people you trust, who have used a specific funeral home, willing to recommend it to you?

Third is cost: Funeral home goods and services should be purchased only in accordance with a realistic assessment of your ability to pay for them. By law, funeral directors must provide cost information over the telephone.

CHOSEN FUNERAL DIRECTOR:

Name_____

Address _____

Phone _____

FUNERAL DIRECTOR—FIRST MEETING

A funeral director provides services and merchandise needed or chosen at the time of a death. Funeral professionals coordinate arrangements and care for the body. Funeral directors ordinarily visit primary survivors in the family home on the day of the death. The dual purpose of this meeting is:

• To discuss with you the services you want the funeral director to provide.

• To obtain from you the information about the deceased that is needed to make the arrangements.

At this time, you will need to make these decisions about the care of the body and the service:

• Do you choose a *memorial service* or a *funeral?*

• Do you choose *cremation* instead of *burial?* (Embalming may not be required.)

• Do you choose *immediate burial without embalming?*

More information to help you make these decisions can be found in the following pages.

The funeral director will need:

- Personal biographical information for the deceased. See the Personal History pages 57-65.

- A list of newspapers and media you want notified (see page 56).

DISCOVERING PREFERENCES
OF THE DECEASED

Survivors usually want to honor the wishes of the deceased. Here are some suggestions for locating some preferences about care for the body and worship services.

- *Remember conversations.* What was said about arrangements and services at the time of a death?

- *Review* what the person did when making arrangements at the death of a parent, a spouse, or a child.

- Is anything *written down* that reflects the wishes of the deceased?

  Check any "precious papers" the deceased saved. Are there "files of memories" somewhere?

  Check favorite reading materials. Look through them for underlining and margin notations.

  Check the person's favorite Bible. Thumb through it. People often tuck cherished clippings in their Bibles, mark favorite passages, and make meaningful margin notes.

  Check the person's will. Specific instructions for services and arrangements are sometimes included in that document.

- *Examine the deceased person's safety deposit box,* if it is accessible, for helpful records.

- Modern technology has created information sources that should not be overlooked. Be sure to check the person's *computer.* Some people also keep notes on *tape recorders.* Check the collection of cassettes, if there is one.

> *Make a joyful noise to the Lord,*
> *all the earth.*
> *Worship the Lord with gladness;*
> *come into his presence with singing.*
> *Know that the Lord is God.*
> *It is he that made us,*
> *and we are his;*
> *we are his people,*
> *and the sheep of his pasture.*
>
>
> PSALM 100:1-3

CARING FOR THE BODY

- Did the deceased person plan the *donation of organs* to aid the living or *body donation* for medical education or research? If yes, turn to medical personnel for guidance.

- Do you choose to have an *autopsy?* Knowing actual causes of death may provide comfort and reassurance. The funeral director and medical personnel will help you with this.

- Have any *advance arrangements* been planned with a particular funeral home?

- Is the deceased a member of a *Memorial Society* which needs to be contacted to assist with arrangements (see page 133)?[1]

- Does the family want to choose the *private option* and care for the burial themselves (see page 133)?[2]

- Did the deceased request or do you choose *cremation* (see pages 92-94)?

- Do you want to have the body *embalmed?* (See the next page.)

EMBALMING

Embalming is the injection of chemicals to retard decay. Embalming, as typically practiced in North America, is solely for *short-term preservation* of the body. The single purpose is to delay decomposition. This makes possible:

- The completion of arrangements and services, which may take several days to accomplish.

- Transportation of the body to another location, if necessary.

- The viewing of the body by family and friends before its final disposition.

Embalmed bodies begin to deteriorate within a week. This degeneration may be slowed by refrigeration.

Routine embalming is not required by any state law. A few states do require embalming if the body is to be transported by common carrier or if death was caused by a communicable or contagious disease. However, there is no reliable scientific evidence proving that embalming prevents the spread of disease.[3]

If there is a physical body,
there is also a spiritual body.

1 CORINTHIANS 15:44B

PASTOR—FIRST MEETING

Ideally, your pastor will have been able to be with you and "walk" with you through *The Choice Guide* up to this point. Of course, understandably, this is not always possible.

The first time you meet with your pastor, answers to these questions will be needed:

- Will you want the church to provide a *family dinner*, either before or after the memorial or funeral service? Is it the congregation's custom to provide such meals? If you choose to have a family dinner, you need to begin determining how many people will be at the dinner. By tomorrow those preparing the meal will need to know how many guests will be coming.

- Will there be a need for a *nursery* for preschool-age children during the memorial or funeral service? (Although children should not be forced to attend the memorial or funeral service, it is psychologically and spiritually healthy for them to be present—unless they are too young to participate.)

- If you choose to have a memorial service—and it may also be done for a funeral service in the church—it is especially appropriate to have *ushers* who are chosen from among friends or church members. The role of the ushers is the same as for a typical Sunday worship service—to greet worshipers and to distribute orders of service.

- It is also appropriate to have friends or church members ask those attending the funeral to sign the *guest book*.

- Often the church's chief usher or the pastor will gladly notify these people and meet with them for instructions. If they are not able to do it, the funeral director may call them and provide direction. Alternatively, you may ask a family member or friend to invite selected individuals to participate.

WORKING LIST FOR POSSIBLE USHERS:

_____ Phone: _____

_____ Phone: _____

_____ Phone: _____

_____ Phone: _____

_____ Phone: _____

_____ Phone: _____

USHERS CHOSEN:

_____ Phone: _____

_____ Phone: _____

_____ Phone: _____

_____ Phone: _____

WORKING LIST FOR POSSIBLE GUEST BOOK ATTENDANTS:

_____ Phone: _____

_____ Phone: _____

_____ Phone: _____

_____ Phone: _____

GUEST BOOK ATTENDANTS CHOSEN:

_____ Phone: _____

_____ Phone: _____

Abide in me as I abide in you....
As the Father has loved me, so I have
loved you; abide in my love.
If you keep my commandments, you will
abide in my love, just as I have kept my
Father's commandments and abide
in his love....
This is my commandment, that
you love one another as I have loved you.

JOHN 15:4a, 9-10, 12

Select another time before the service to meet with your pastor and make specific plans for the worship service. Sometimes this may be one day before the service in order to allow time for everyone to arrive whom you may wish to have participate in these choices.

Consider including in this meeting with the pastor as many family members as possible. You also may include "close-like-family" friends. This meeting may include as few as three people, and as many as forty.

Hold this meeting with the pastor in the church, if possible. During the days immediately following a death, purposeful conversation and opportunities for thoughtful choices are almost impossible at the family home. There are too many interruptions with the phone ringing and caring people coming and going. If the church is not a possibility, consider using a community building or other room available to the public.

TIME FOR NEXT MEETING WITH THE PASTOR:

Day _____ Time _____

Place _____

(You also may make note of this in the appointment schedule, page 141.)

MUSICIANS

(Note: See pages 109-110, Music in the Service.)

If you want particular musicians to participate in the memorial or funeral service, they need to be informed and invited to take part as soon as possible.

The funeral director usually talks with musicians. However, a family member or the pastor may communicate with the musicians if a more personal approach is preferred.

Soloist(s): _____

_____

Organist: _____

Pianist: _____

Other musicians: _____

Your Special Music Requests:

_____

_____

_____

_____

_____

DO WHAT IS RIGHT FOR YOU

The repeated advice of people who have made arrangements at the time of a death is, "Do what is right for you." *It is not necessary to be bound by tradition.*

It is OK if you choose arrangements that are different from the norm, from local customs and traditions. Over and over, people who have been through this experience recommend that you "take the freedom to do what is right for you and your family." They say, "Do what is helpful to *you*, what comforts *you*."

It is easy to be controlled by our perceptions of other people's expectations. It is important to make your own choices and not be governed by what other people think or by your impressions of public opinion. Our impressions and perceptions are often incorrect.

If the funeral professionals are hesitant or seem to be resisting your wishes, if they try to change your mind or oppose your requests—*hold your ground*. You are employing their services.

Make choices that are appropriate for your family, for you, and for the person who has died. You can individualize and personalize your arrangements in ways such as the following:

- You may choose to have a private committal service—with family and close friends only—followed by a memorial service.

- A man does not have to be dressed in a business suit and tie when he is placed in a casket for viewing. Dress him as he lived.

- A member of the family may give a eulogy.

- You can choose music and musical instruments for the service that reflect the life of the deceased.

- You can involve family members in other ways; they may participate by providing music or reading poetry or Scripture.

> *Do what you think is right. Do not worry about what other people think. I wish I had done that.*

PLACE FOR THE SERVICE

Because funerals and memorial services are obser-
vances of Christian worship, the most appropriate place
for them is the church, whenever possible. *In a church,
symbols of the faith, not the casket, provide the center of
worship.* If the service is held in the funeral home or a
private home, include customary symbols of Christian
worship such as a cross, candles, and a Bible. Sing
hymns to encourage the mourners' faith in God's care
and in eternal life, perhaps including favorite hymns of
the deceased.

CHOSEN PLACE FOR FUNERAL/MEMORIAL SERVICE:

_____

_____

_____

A MEMORIAL SERVICE OR A FUNERAL?

- A service is called a *funeral* when the *body is present*.

- If the *body is not present*, it is called a *memorial service*.

Except for the presence or absence of the body, funerals and memorial services are typically very similar.

- The *committal service*—often informally called a "graveside service"—and burial (or cremation or body donation) occur *after a funeral service*.

Committal services may follow the funeral immediately, or may be a day or more later if burial is to be at a distance.

- The *committal service* and final caring for the remains occur *before a memorial service*.

The choice of a memorial service makes possible options which are not practical or are awkward with a funeral service.

OPTIONS MADE POSSIBLE
BY A MEMORIAL SERVICE

If you choose to have a memorial service, it is *simpler to plan a private graveside committal service* in the special intimacy of family and selected friends. A committal service may be prior to a memorial service on the same day. But it doesn't need to be on the same day. A memorial service may be the day after, or even several days or weeks following a committal service.

A memorial service enables you to choose the *most practical and convenient time* for gathering your family and friends. Since the body has already been cared for, the choice of a service time is not restricted by mortuary staff schedules, daylight hours of cemeteries, weekend overtime rates of cemetery personnel, or cemeteries closed on weekends and holidays. For the convenience of those who cannot get time off from their jobs, a memorial service may be scheduled, for example, on an evening or on a Sunday afternoon.

The feeling of a memorial service is frequently *more relaxed, open, and comfortable* because the finality of the burial, or other disposition of the remains, has been completed. Following a memorial service, the family may greet people who attended the service in the church fellowship hall or foyer. Often a church will provide appropriate refreshments to create a pleasant reception-like atmosphere. Some families will ask the church to provide refreshments for this reception time instead of a family dinner.

Christians celebrate the resurrection—that God is forever giving new life, both in this life and in life beyond death. Because final caring for the body is completed prior to a memorial service, we may be *more inclined to hear the healing word of new life* and respond in faith.

TIME FOR THE SERVICE

Whether you are planning a funeral service or a memorial service, you will need to keep these points in mind:

- The family, pastor, and funeral director *must all agree* on a time before it is announced.

- Consider times to allow the *greatest number* of people to participate. Think about:

  Travel plans of those coming from distances.

  Work schedules of those who may want to participate.

  An evening service is convenient for people who cannot get time off work. This is practical if a memorial service is chosen or if burial will be at a distance on a different day.

  A late afternoon service—4:00 P.M. or after—as an option for teachers and others who may get off work a little early.

A Sunday afternoon service is an option that may meet the needs of both family and friends and is especially compatible with a memorial service.

TYPE OF SERVICE AND TIMES

Type of service:

      _____ Funeral   _____ Memorial service
            Possible times:

_____ Day _____ Time

_____ Day _____ Time

_____ Day _____Time

Chosen time for funeral/memorial service:

_____ Day _____Time

Possible committal (graveside) service times:

_____ Day _____Time

_____ Day _____Time

_____ Day _____Time

Chosen committal (graveside) service time:

_____ Day (after the funeral)
                      or
_____ Day _____Time

IF YOU MUST MAKE ARRANGEMENTS
IN AN UNFAMILIAR PLACE

If the death occurred in a city other than the one in which you live, and you must come from out of town to make arrangements for a funeral or memorial service, there are a few things you can do to make your job easier.

For burials and funerals to be made in the same city where the death occurred. Either before or immediately upon your arrival in town, take the initiative to telephone the pastor and the church. If you make arrangements in a community other than where you reside, check with the deceased's church—or other friends and associates of the deceased—to locate a reputable funeral director.

Once you have chosen a funeral director, establish contact with him (or her) soon after your arrival in the city where the funeral is to be held. Let the director know who you are, and where and when you can be reached. Ask for a time to meet together with the pastor.

When you seek recommendations for musicians or need information about local customs, do not solely depend on funeral industry professionals; you may want to ask the pastor. You may find a consultant-friend among the friends and associates of the deceased.

When burial occurs in a community different from the funeral service, the funeral director at the point of origin normally arranges for the burial. The funeral director usually networks with a funeral director in the community where burial occurs. Ask for a detailed itemization of costs for these special arrangements and transportation of the body. If someone dies and you are traveling overseas with them, seek help from the American consulate in the foreign country *and* contact your local hometown funeral director.

A PLAIN PINE BOX?

Homemade burial boxes—of pine or plywood—are easy to build if family members or friends want to make them. Simple "do it yourself" instructions are available. Check your public library or your church library. For easily followed plans see: Ernest Morgan, *Dealing Creatively with Death: A Manual of Death Education and Simple Burial,* Twelfth Revised Edition (Bayside, N.Y.: Barclay, 1990), pages 111-114.

REQUESTING "NO FLOWERS"

Some families—for personal reasons or by request of the deceased—will prefer to minimize flowers at the service. *Most newspapers will not print a "no flowers" request except in paid obituaries.* By word of mouth, the family may suggest:

"The family requests no flowers, please."

or

"The family prefers no flowers, please."

MEMORIAL GIFTS—SUGGESTED CHARITIES OR INSTITUTIONS

The family customarily selects charities or institutions that are suggested as recipients for memorial gifts. Choices often are special interests of the deceased or characteristic concerns and interests of the person. Examples are: a church memorial fund, medical research, and hospices.

SUGGESTIONS—MEMORIAL GIFTS

_____

_____

_____

_____

_____

NEWSPAPER OBITUARY NOTIFICATION

Most newspapers have fixed guidelines governing what they will include in obituaries. Many newspapers only accept obituary information when it is reported by a funeral director. Some newspapers only print paid obituaries.

What newspapers need to be notified? In what cities, towns, or regions has the person lived?

Newspaper Name: _____

City or Town: _____

Newspaper Name: _____

City or Town: _____

Newspaper Name: _____

City or Town: _____

Newspaper Name: _____

City or Town: _____

Newspaper Name: _____

City or Town: _____

Newspaper Name: _____

City or Town: _____

PERSONAL HISTORY

The funeral director will ask for vital biographical data about the deceased. *This information is necessary for the completion of the death certificate and other legal documents.* It is also the basis for *obituary notifications* provided for the news media.

PERSONAL INFORMATION

Full name: _____

Address: _____

City: _____

County : _____ State: _____

Date resided at this location: since _____

Social Security number: _____

BIRTH AND PARENTAGE

Birthday: Month _____ Day _____ Year _____

Age: _____

Place of Birth: _____

City: _____ County : _____

State: _____ Country : _____

Father's name: _____

Father's place of birth: _____

Father's residence: _____

Father deceased?   Yes____   No____

Mother's maiden name: _____

Mother's place of birth: _____

Mother's residence: _____

Mother deceased?   Yes____   No____

Stepfather's name: _____

Deceased?   Yes____   No____

Stepmother's name: _____

Deceased?   Yes____   No____

MARITAL STATUS

Single: ____   Married: ____   Widowed: ____   Divorced: ____

Spouse's name: _____

Wife's maiden name: _____

Date of marriage: _____

Place of marriage: _____

Previous marriages: _____

(Note: A copy of a marriage license will be
needed when filing insurance claims.)

MILITARY SERVICE

Military serial number: _____

Branch of service: _____

Rank: _____

Dates of service: _____

Veterans' Administration claim number:

_____

*(Note: Military discharge papers will be
required for filing claims.)*

CHILDREN

Name: _____

Residence: _____

Name: _____

Residence: _____

Name: _____

Residence: _____

Name: _____

Residence: _____

Name: _____

Residence: _____

STEPCHILDREN

Name: _____

Residence: _____

Name: _____

Residence: _____

Name: _____

Residence: _____

Name: _____

Residence: _____

SISTERS AND BROTHERS

Name: _____

Residence: _____

Name: _____

Residence: _____

Name: _____

Residence: _____

Name: _____

Residence: _____

Name: _____

Residence: _____

OTHER IMMEDIATE FAMILY
(STEPFAMILY MEMBERS, ETC.)

Name: _____ Relationship: _____

Residence: _____

Name: _____ Relationship: _____

Residence: _____

Name: _____ Relationship: _____

Residence: _____

Name: _____ Relationship: _____

Residence: _____

Name: _____ Relationship: _____

Residence: _____

Name: _____ Relationship: _____

Residence: _____

PREVIOUS RESIDENCES

Dates: _____ Location: _____

Dates: _____ Location: _____

Dates: _____ Location: _____

Dates: _____ Location: _____

SCHOOLS ATTENDED

School: _____ Dates attended: _____

Degree or Certificate/Honors Earned: _____

_____

School: _____ Dates attended: _____

Degree or Certificate/Honors Earned: _____

_____

School: _____ Dates attended: _____

Degree or Certificate/Honors Earned: _____

_____

School: _____ Dates attended: _____

Degree or Certificate/Honors Earned: _____

_____

EMPLOYMENT RECORD

Occupation (previous if retired): _____

Employer (or retired from): _____

Previous Employers

Name of Company/Occupation: _____

Location: _____ Dates: _____

Name of Company/Occupation: _____

Location: _____ Dates: _____

Name of Company/Occupation: _____

Location: _____ Dates: _____

Name of Company/Occupation: _____

Location: _____ Dates: _____

Name of Company/Occupation: _____

Location: _____ Dates: _____

Organizations and Memberships

_____

_____

_____

_____

_____

CHURCH AFFILIATION

Name of congregation: _____

Location: _____

Record of service in the church:

_____

_____

_____

_____

_____

COMMUNITY AND VOLUNTEER SERVICE

_____

_____

_____

_____

_____

_____

_____

_____

ACCOMPLISHMENTS AND HONORS

_____

_____

_____

_____

_____

_____

_____

_____

ADDITIONAL INFORMATION

_____

_____

_____

_____

_____

_____

_____

_____

SECOND ROUND OF NOTIFICATIONS

Once service times have been set, begin the second round of notifications to persons who live at a distance. Many of these telephone calls may be made for you by friends and family members.

TAKE CARE OF YOURSELF

Do what you need to do to take care of yourself right now during these difficult and demanding days. Make time for yourself in whatever way is most helpful for you. Let someone else answer the phone and the door and take messages. Turn off the ringer on your telephone. Make "space" for yourself whenever you need it.

If one member suffers, all suffer together with it; if one member is honored, all rejoice together with it.
Now you are the body of Christ and individually members of it.

1 CORINTHIANS 12:26-27

CHECKLIST

☐ Choose a trusted consultant-friend (page 22)

☐ Call your pastor as soon as possible (pages 23 and 41)

☐ Begin a "to do later" list (pages 23 and 137)

☐ List people to notify (pages 25-31)

☐ Choose a funeral director (pages 34 and 35)

☐ Decide how to care for the body (pages 39 and 40)

☐ Choose a place for the service (page 48)

☐ Choose the type of service—funeral or memorial service (pages 49-51)

☐ Plan times for the services (pages 51-52)

☐ If you must make arrangements in an unfamiliar place (page 53)

☐ Plan other details:

    ☐ Consider the preferences of the deceased (page 37)

    ☐ First meeting with pastor (page 41)

    ☐ Ushers (pages 42)

    ☐ Musicians (page 45)

    ☐ A plain pine box? (page 54)

    ☐ "No flowers?" (page 54)

    ☐ Memorial gifts? (page 55)

☐ Record personal history for newspaper obituary and legal documents (pages 57-65)

☐ Complete second round of notifications (page 66)

*But we have this treasure in clay jars, so that it
may be made clear that this extraordinary
power belongs to God and does not come
from us.*

*We are afflicted in every way, but not crushed;
perplexed, but not driven to despair; perse-
cuted, but not forsaken; struck down, but
not destroyed....*

So we do not lose heart.

*Even though our outer nature is wasting away,
our inner nature is being renewed day by
day....*

*We look not at what can be seen but at what
cannot be seen; for what can be seen is tem-
porary, but what cannot be seen is eternal.*

2 Corinthians 4:7-9, 16, 18

The Day After the Death

⚜

CHECK YOUR PERSONAL FINANCES IMMEDIATELY

Check your short-term financial situation—if you have not already done so—for *personal living expenses.*

Next, evaluate your monetary resources for the *expenses of arrangements* you choose. Some arrangements may require immediate payment. Some fees, such as those for opening and closing a grave, must be paid in advance.

Choose and set a maximum amount that you are able to spend for funeral expenses. Carefully and thoroughly discuss this amount with family members *before* you visit the funeral home to select the casket as well as other merchandise and services. Ask other family members to help you stay within the predetermined limit you set.

INCLUDE YOUR FAMILY

Whenever possible and appropriate, include your family—spouse, children, brothers, sisters—in the decision-making process. Including them not only provides emotional support and counsel for you, it also helps their grieving to begin in a healthier way. It may be appropriate and helpful also to include very close friends—especially your "trusted consultant-friend."

PREPARING FOR YOUR VISIT TO THE FUNERAL HOME TO MAKE CHOICES

Experience is a practical and wise teacher. Experience suggests:

- Family members need to discuss the cost of the casket and the expense for the services prior to going to the funeral home. It is best to *choose a price range—a set dollar maximum limit—before* the family goes to the funeral home to make selections. Because of the effects of emotional shock, this is not a good time for making financial decisions.

- Expenses you will need to consider are discussed on pages 75-79. Worksheets for an Expense Itemization and Summary are on pages 80-83.

- Throughout the process of choosing merchandise and arrangements, ask yourself:

  1. Are these financial decisions consistent with the values of the person who died?

2. Are these choices consistent with the personal financial value system I use in normal circumstances? Are these choices compatible with my ordinary beliefs about substantial economic decisions?

Here is some advice from people who have "been there":

> *"Stop and think about what is important to you. Who are you really doing this for? Remember your value system in ordinary times."*

> *"I asked lots of questions; lots and lots of questions. If you cannot ask the questions, get someone to ask them for you."*

> *"Check out the 'stories' you have heard. They may be incorrect and based on misinformation. We had been told a service at the church costs more. It does not and it shouldn't."*

ASK YOUR TRUSTED CONSULTANT-FRIEND TO GO WITH YOU TO THE FUNERAL HOME

Your trusted consultant-friend can *ask questions without embarrassment* and provide you with steady and needed psychological support. Your friend can ask questions you and family members emotionally may not be able to ask.

Your trusted consultant-friend will *help you remember* your basic values and think clearly—and will be less vulnerable than you are to the sophisticated sales and merchandising techniques used by some funeral directors.

If you did not choose a "trusted consultant-friend"—or that person is unable to go with you and your family, perhaps another friend or your pastor can go with you.

CASH-ADVANCE ITEMS

"Cash-advance items" are things a funeral director purchases or pays for on behalf of the consumer.

Examples of cash-advance items that might be paid for by the funeral director are as follows: honoraria for a soloist, organist, or other musician; flowers; paid obituary notices in newspapers; honoraria for clergy.

Many funeral providers simply charge their cost for these items. Some charge a fee for performing these services. The Funeral Rule of the Federal Trade Commission mandates that funeral providers inform the consumer when a service fee is added or if the provider gets a refund, discount, or rebate from any supplier of cash-advance items.[4]

COST ITEMIZATION

Federal regulations require itemized price disclosures by funeral directors—whether requested or not—before arrangements are finally completed.

Phone requests for price information are a good idea. These figures are needed when the family discusses costs while choosing an agreed-upon price range—a set maximum dollar limit. The funeral director is *required by federal regulations to provide price information by telephone.* If funeral industry personnel are reluctant to give you cost figures—or try to talk you into waiting until you visit the funeral home—remind them that they are required by federal regulations to furnish price details by telephone.

A consumer protection rule regulating funeral industry practices went into effect April 30, 1984 (Federal Trade Commission).[5] It assures your right to:

- obtain information about funeral arrangements by telephone or in person;
- a written price list of goods and services available, including *each* individual item and service offered;
- select only the goods and services needed or wanted;
- pay only for the merchandise and services chosen.

CEMETERY—EARTH BURIAL

In North America, the most common form of final care for the body is earth burial. *Grave plots vary in cost* from as little as $100 (or less) in rural public cemeteries to $600 (or more) in urban commercial cemeteries. Rural graveyards usually are publicly owned (by the city, township, or county) and nonprofit. Many in metropolitan regions are owned by for-profit corporations.

Churches also may have cemeteries. Some states permit family burying grounds on privately owned land.

Payment in advance may be required for opening and closing the grave.

Gravestones. Traditional cemeteries allow families to choose any gravestone. Many newer commercial "memorial parks" require the stones to be level with the ground. It is often wise to delay purchase of a gravestone until other funeral expenses are paid.

Cemetery policies. Cemeteries may have policies restricting plantings around the grave and the type of monuments permitted. There also may be other limits. Some cemeteries require that monuments be purchased only through them.

Grave liners are required by most cemeteries. Their only purpose is to prevent settling—over time—of the ground above the grave as the body decomposes and the casket deteriorates. This reduces maintenance of the cemetery grounds. A sealed liner does not prevent or slow decomposition. The sealing of a grave liner serves no realistic functional purpose.

The most basic grave liner—and the least expensive— is made of concrete slabs assembled on the site. A coffin vault is a one-piece unit made of concrete, metal or fiberglass. A liner or vault is lowered by machine into the grave excavation.

Maintenance fees. In some cases maintenance fees must be paid each year. Other times they may be included in the grave cost, be paid in a lump sum, or be paid for by taxes.

Burial cost information. Burial cost information may be secured from the funeral director or by directly contacting the cemetery office or the responsible governmental unit (city, township, or county). *Be sure to secure a written copy of policies from the cemetery.*

BURIAL COST SUMMARY:

Grave plot . . . .$_____

Opening and closing the grave . . . . . $_____

Extra charge for weekends
and holidays (if allowed) . . . .$_____

Grave liner (or vault) . . . . $_____

Grave marker or stone . . . . $_____

Maintenance fees . . . .$_____

Total . . . .$_____

CASKET SELECTION

Most funeral providers courteously and graciously leave the family alone in the casket selection room to make their choice without inappropriate pressure or influence.

If funeral service personnel remain in the casket selection room with you, gently but firmly ask them to leave. This is a personal, private family time. If you have questions, you can ask them to return to the room.

Negotiate the final cost. If it is your normal way to dicker and haggle over a price, there is no reason not to do so. The mark-up on caskets often is 300 percent and even up to 500 percent or more.[6] The funeral director has "room" to negotiate. Someone who did so says, "There is no reason not to 'bargain.' I did. I thought the price was too high."

If the total cost is too much for your set price range, and if you cannot negotiate an acceptable figure, make alternative choices by leaving out options or choosing a different casket.

The casket is the major variable expense in the average funeral.[7]

OPTIONAL GOODS AND SERVICES FROM THE FUNERAL DIRECTOR

The Federal Trade Commission rule regulating the funeral industry requires the funeral provider to furnish a single statement itemizing the individual services and merchandise being considered for purchase. This makes possible the addition or subtraction of items for choosing only what is wanted.[8]

These items, for example, might be considered for possible exclusion:

- *Funeral home cars.* Do you need the funeral home cars for the family? Or will family members drive their own cars?

- *Thank you notes* and *guest books.* As a convenience, funeral homes routinely provide thank you notes and guest books. They probably can be purchased for less from other sources. Personally purchasing thank you notes allows the choice of cards to match your individual taste.

- *Memorial folders.* If your congregation provides a printed worship order, funeral home "memorial folders" are unnecessary. All of the information may be included in the worship bulletin.

EXPENSE ITEMIZATION AND SUMMARY

The following pages provide—in one place—a summary of all the expenses related to final caring for the body and service of worship. Some items may not apply for you.

CARE FOR THE BODY

Removal of remains . . . .$_____

Embalming . . . .$_____

Cosmetic preparation . . . .$_____

Hairdresser . . . .$_____

Other . . . .$_____

FACILITIES

Use of viewing room . . . .$_____

Use of funeral home chapel . . . .$_____
    (NOTE: Churches *do not charge*
    church members user fees for funerals
    or memorial services.)
Other facilities:

_____ . . . .$_____

_____ . . . .$_____

_____ . . . .$_____

VEHICLES

Use of hearse . . . .$_____

Use of one limousine . . . .$_____

Use of each additional limousine . . . .$_____

Flower car or truck . . . .$_____

FILINGS

Death certificate . . . .$_____

Death certificate copies . . . .$_____

Burial permit . . . .$_____

Arranging for the death notice . . . . . .$_____

Filing for death benefits . . . .$_____

Paid newspaper obituary . . . .$_____

Other filings:

_____ . . . .$_____

PROFESSIONAL SERVICES

Funeral home staff . . . .$_____

Soloist . . . .$_____

Organist . . . .$_____

Other musicians . . . .$_____

Service fees, cash-advance items, etc. . .$_____

Other services:

_____ . . . .$_____

MERCHANDISE

Casket . . . .$_____
(Before completing your casket
selection, read "A Pall" on page 121).

Thank you notes . . . .$_____

Guest book(s) . . . .$_____

Memorial folders . . . .$_____

Other items:

_____ . . . .$_____

_____ . . . .$_____

CEMETERY

Purchase of gravesite . . . .$_____

Cemetery maintenance fee,
if additional . . . .$_____

Opening and closing the grave . . . . .$_____

Additional charge for weekend or
holiday grave opening and closing .$_____

Grave liner (or vault) . . . .$_____

Grave marker or stone . . . .$_____

CREMATION

Cost of cremation . . . .$_____

Container for the body . . . .$_____

Transportation of the body
   to the crematory . . . .$_____

Shipping of cremains . . . .$_____

Urn (if needed) . . . .$_____

Medical examiner fee (if required) . . .$_____

OTHER OPTIONS

Flowers from the family . . . .$_____

Gift to the church . . . .$_____

Honoraria for clergy . . . .$_____

Additional Items:

_____ . . . .$_____

_____ . . . .$_____

_____ . . . .$_____

_____ . . . .$_____

_____ . . . .$_____

_____ . . . .$_____

TOTAL COST . . . .$_____

DEATH CERTIFICATE COPIES

The funeral director will ask how many copies of the death certificate you will need. The funeral home will order additional copies of the death certificate for you when it files the official forms.

You will need more copies of the death certificate than you anticipate. In most states, it is most cost-effective—as well as convenient—to order extra copies of the death certificate at this time. They are required for insurance claims, pensions, property title changes, and investments—just to name a few things. Estimate the number of death certificates you will need based on the deceased's number of investments, properties, pensions, and insurance policies.

Several experienced survivors recommend beginning with one dozen as a minimum. The cost is modest and the convenience of not having to reorder is an advantage. Reorders typically require another "first copy" charge, which makes them more expensive. One survivor said, "I was surprised how many copies of the death certificate I needed. I used at least fifteen."

CLOTHING FOR THE BODY

When selecting clothing for the body, be sure to include *glasses* if the person normally wore them. Shoes are not needed.

You may ask the funeral director, before the coffin is finally closed, to remove rings, glasses, and jewelry.

You may dress the person as he or she lived—rather than "dressing them up." As one person said, "I wanted to dress Daddy as he lived. He hated suits and ties!"

A young widow said, "I wanted to dress my husband in the clothes in which he lived and worked. This was his request. I was hesitant because of 'what other people might think,' but I was encouraged to dress his body as he wanted. I am glad that I did."

Take the freedom to make choices that are appropriate for you.

VIEWING FOR THE FAMILY

Each family member—at a time best for the individual—is well advised to view the body. As difficult as this is to do, it is important for emotional and spiritual recovery. Viewing the body helps begin the healing of the tearing pain death causes.

Facing the stark reality of death is necessary for recovery and healing to begin. Long-term denial of death blocks recovery and healing.

Often we will hear, "But I want to remember her as she was." And we do remember special people as they were. It also is important, for the health of the living, that we remember clearly that the person is dead.

There is no "right" or "wrong" way for family members to view the body. Each person needs to do it the way that is best for him or her. Some families go in groups. Some go one or two at a time. If someone in your family insists on not viewing the body, allow them that freedom. It may be their way of grieving and not denial. Do what is best for you, and encourage your family members to do the same.

VISITATION FOR THE PUBLIC

The reasons for a visitation opportunity for friends and acquaintances are the same as those for viewing by the family.

In circumstances when viewing is not possible—for example, when the body is badly disfigured in an accident—an appropriate and tasteful alternative is to display a picture of the deceased at the funeral or memorial service.

Public visitation may take place in these ways:

- First, a time may be publicly announced when the *family will receive and greet callers* at the funeral home. (Families may choose *not* to have a time when they greet callers at the funeral home.)

- Second, the *casket may be open prior to a funeral service* in the church foyer or in a funeral home viewing room or lobby. (It is preferable not to do this at the front of the church or funeral home "chapel," where the casket might replace the symbols of the faith as the focus of worship.)

- Third, there may be announced times when people, at their *convenience,* may stop by the funeral home.

- Fourth, all three forms of visitation noted above may be provided—or any combination of two of them.

Public visitation and viewing

Will the public be invited to stop at the funeral home and to view the remains?

Yes _____   No _____

Will the casket be open for viewing in the church foyer or funeral home viewing room or lobby prior to the funeral service?

Yes _____   No _____

If the family chooses to greet and receive people at a visitation time in the funeral home, when will that be?

Day _____

Time: From _____ to _____

PALLBEARERS

Six pallbearers are usually chosen, although up to eight may be used.

Women may be pallbearers. A mix of men and women may be chosen. Three or four husband and wife couples may be selected.

Persons selected to be pallbearers need to be physically capable of helping to lift the weight of the coffin.

Honorary pallbearers. Personal respect and appreciation by recognition as honorary pallbearers may be granted special people and those who are physically not able to be active pallbearers. *As many honorary pallbearers may be acknowledged as the family chooses.* For more information, see the next heading.

Choosing and asking pallbearers. Generally the common procedure is for the funeral director to phone the people you choose and ask them to serve as pallbearers. If you wish to personalize the invitations to be pallbearers, a family member or a special friend could contact them.

WORKING LIST FOR POSSIBLE ACTIVE PALLBEARERS:

_____ Phone_____

_____ Phone_____

_____ Phone_____

_____ Phone_____

_____ Phone_____

_____ Phone_____

_____ Phone_____

_____ Phone_____

_____ Phone_____

_____ Phone_____

_____ Phone_____

_____ Phone_____

_____ Phone_____

PALLBEARERS CHOSEN:

1. _____ Phone_____

2. _____ Phone_____

3. _____ Phone_____

4. _____ Phone_____

5. _____ Phone_____

6. _____ Phone_____

And, if you wish:

7. _____ Phone_____

8. _____ Phone_____

ALTERNATE PALLBEARER CHOICES—
IF ANY OF THE PEOPLE LISTED ABOVE ARE NOT AVAILABLE:

1. _____ Phone_____

2. _____ Phone_____

3. _____ Phone_____

4. _____ Phone_____

HONORARY PALLBEARERS

Honorary pallbearers ordinarily sit together at the funeral or memorial service.

Funeral directors typically phone these persons and ask them to serve as honorary pallbearers. You may wish to personalize the invitation to be an honorary pallbearer by having a family member or a special friend make the contact.

HONORARY PALLBEARERS:

1. _____ Phone_____

2. _____ Phone_____

3. _____ Phone_____

4. _____ Phone_____

5. _____ Phone_____

6. _____ Phone_____

7. _____ Phone_____

8. _____ Phone_____

9. _____ Phone_____

CREMATION

Often cremation is a request of the deceased. The cremation process returns the body to the elements through intense heat and evaporation.

Cremains are clean and white and may be stored indefinitely.[9] "Cremains" is a more accurate term than "ashes." Cremains are the three to seven pounds of small bone fragments remaining after the cremation process.[10] Most crematories pulverize the fragments into small granular particles. Only mineral content remains.[11]

The time required for cremation depends on the time it takes to transport the body to the crematory and return the cremains to the family.

Crematories put the cremains in cardboard, tin, or plastic containers. These are for transportation purposes. They may be shipped by registered mail or by some (but not all) express delivery services.

Usually embalming is not needed before cremation. If the body must be transported to a crematory, embalming may be required by regulations in a few states.

A casket is not necessary. The funeral director may provide an inexpensive nonmetal, rigid, and combustible container for transportation of the remains to the crematory. These are made of pressboard or fiberboard, cardboard, canvas, or wood. They are often labelled "alternative containers."

Funeral directors have decorative urns for sale. Alternatively, the family may wish to use a receptacle already in their possession. One family put the cremains in beautiful wooden vases which had been handmade by the deceased, a highly skilled and respected craftsman. Before you buy a commercially provided urn, you might consider ways of providing a more personalized vessel.

The cremains also may be kept in the cardboard, tin, or plastic container provided by the crematory. Our family kept my father's cremains this way for several months until we could distribute them at a favorite mountain location during a vacation trip.

Direct cremation customarily costs significantly less than earth burial. However, funeral directors' charges for transportation and paperwork may be more than the cost of the cremation.[12]

DISTRIBUTION OF CREMAINS

Often the deceased, in conversation, will have given a general idea where he or she would prefer for the cremains to be distributed.

Often, cremains are scattered in places of special meaning to the deceased or the family. They may be spread at a favorite park, garden, or woods—at sea, on a lake, or from a mountaintop. The possibilities are limited only by your imagination. Cremains also may be buried.

Only California restricts disposition of cremated remains. In California, cremains may be scattered at sea, buried in a cemetery, or kept at a home.

If the family does not want to personally participate

in spreading the cremains, they may ask someone else—a friend or pastor—to do so for them. One pastor recalls a gorgeous Easter Sunday afternoon when—near a place where the deceased had played as a child—he cast the cremains of a parishioner off a bridge into a river below.

FLOWERS FROM THE FAMILY

Flowers symbolize life in the midst of death. The immediate family of the deceased person customarily provides a special flower arrangement for the service. Occasionally, a family chooses not to honor this custom and use the funds saved for a memorial gift.

It is important to *set a price limit*—to decide in advance what you will spend. These options for flowers are suggested:

- The family may provide a *casket piece*—a flower spray or floral blanket.

- The family may provide a *basket* or an *arrangement* of flowers.

- Some members of the family can make your own flower arrangement.

(See the information about "A Pall" on page 121. When a pall is used, floral sprays or blankets are not placed on the casket.)

These ideas may be helpful to you:

"We placed an Indian blanket from a mission of our church on the casket. Instead of buying flowers, we gave the money to the mission."

"We made our own flower arrangements. We used wildflowers from the mountains where Dad lived. We created several arrangements. This made the flowers for the service very personal."

SPECIAL REQUESTS AND SPECIFIC INSTRUCTIONS

If ways of doing things are chosen which vary from the funeral director's standard routine:

- Your desires and instructions need to be very specific and clear.

- You may have to remind the director (or staff) of your specific special requests.

For example:

- If you want the casket to be lowered into the grave during the committal service, while mourners are present, you must specifically make this request.

- If the family wants to stay following the committal service to be present and observe while the grave is closed, this will need to be a special request.

- If the family chooses to participate in closing the grave—at least in symbolic ways, for example, by throwing handfuls or shovelfuls of dirt into the grave—this will require definite and clear instructions.

- If the committal service is first, prior to a memorial service, it is important to say clearly and specifically if you want pallbearers to carry the casket to the grave. You will also need to indicate whether you want this to be part of the ceremony when the family is present. If so, remind the director that the casket is not to be taken to the gravesite until the family is present.

- When a memorial service is chosen, ushering and greeting is appropriately a gift of caring done by church members and friends. It is healthy for them and provides a feeling of community and support. You will need to specifically instruct the funeral professionals to refrain from ushering and greeting at the memorial service. Our family did this before the memorial service for my father. We invited the funeral professionals to attend as our guests. Although our request was unusual for them, they honored our wishes.

The funeral director's role for a memorial service is to remain "in the background," to be in good taste. The primary function of funeral industry personnel at the church is to care for flowers that have been sent as memorial gifts. The funeral director may also help with internal "traffic flow," make sure doors are opened and closed, and place guest books. Remember, and remind your funeral professionals, that church personnel, both ordained and lay volunteers, regularly lead and direct worship services without outside assistance.

OTHER SPECIAL REQUESTS AND INSTRUCTIONS:

_____

_____

_____

_____

_____

_____

A Reminder… If the funeral industry professionals hesitate or resist—if they try to change your mind or oppose your requests—*hold your ground*. You are employing their services.

ACCOMMODATIONS FOR FAMILY AND FRIENDS FROM OUT OF TOWN

What accommodation arrangements do you need to help make for friends and family from out of town? Where might they stay? Private homes? Motels? Hotels?

PEOPLE FOR WHOM YOU NEED TO
HELP LOCATE ACCOMMODATIONS:

_____

_____

_____

_____

PLACES WHERE THEY MIGHT STAY:

_____

_____

_____

_____

If the church or friends do not bring in food, then you will also need to have someone plan for food and meals.

A FAMILY REUNION

Effectively, gatherings for funerals and memorial services are reunions of families and friends.

Consideration needs to be given to making ways for the "family reunion" to happen—for family and friends to gather and visit. Remembering, sharing, and telling stories provides support, encouragement, and healing—the very special gifts given by these gatherings.

Some suggestions:

- One family suggests renting a room at a motel or hotel for a round-the-clock gathering place for the family and friends.

- One family shared that no one in their family still lived where their mother lived and died. This made the visitation time at the funeral home especially meaningful and helpful.

- A memorial service provides the natural and comfortable option of a reception-like time following the memorial service. This gathering may be in the church parish hall—the social or fellowship hall.

- After a funeral service, delay departure for the cemetery and the burial service. Take time to greet friends and guests at the church before going to the cemetery. This may be in the foyer, the parish's social or fellowship hall, in a courtyard, or, if the weather permits, outside in front of the church. Many who attend a funeral service will not or cannot go to the cemetery. Weather often makes the cemetery an inappropriate place to greet friends.

- The family dinner given by the church may be after the formal services are completed. Providers of these meals note that families are more open and relaxed and share more freely when the meal follows the services. They report that when the dinner follows the services, "the family has a more pleasant 'family reunion-type' gathering."

- If there is a traditional funeral with burial following, invite family and friends either to a home or the church for a reunion time.

Times and places that will encourage the "happening" of a reunion of family and friends:

_____

_____

_____

_____

> *A friend loves at all times,*
> *and kinsfolk are born to share adversity.*
>
>
>
> PROVERBS 17:17

CHECKLIST

- ☐ CHECK YOUR PERSONAL FINANCES IMMEDIATELY (page 71)

- ☐ REMEMBER TO INCLUDE YOUR FAMILY (page 71)

- ☐ PREPARE FOR YOUR VISIT TO THE FUNERAL HOME TO MAKE CHOICES (pages 72-73)

  - ☐ Ask family and consultant-friend to go with you (page 74)

  - ☐ Obtain itemized cost list (pages 74-83)

- ☐ CEMETERY: EARTH BURIAL (pages 76-77)

  - ☐ Summarize burial costs (page 77)

  - ☐ Make casket selection (page 78)

  - ☐ Make other decisions

- ☐ DECIDE ABOUT OPTIONAL GOODS AND SERVICES FROM THE FUNERAL DIREC-TOR (page 79)

- ☐ ORDER DEATH CERTIFICATE COPIES (page 84)

- ☐ PROVIDE CLOTHING FOR THE BODY (page 84)

☐ PLAN VIEWING FOR THE FAMILY (page 85)

☐ PLAN VISITATION FOR THE PUBLIC
(page 86)

☐ CHOOSE PALLBEARERS (pages 88-90)

  ☐ Choose honorary pallbearers (page 91)

☐ CREMATION (pages 92-94)

  ☐ Discuss distribution of cremains (page 93)

☐ ORDER FLOWERS FROM THE FAMILY
(page 94)

Do not let your hearts be troubled.
Believe in God, believe also in me. In
my Father's house there are many
dwelling places. If it were not so, would
I have told you that I go to prepare a
place for you? And if I go and prepare a
place for you, I will come again and
will take you to myself, so that where I
am, there you may be also.

JOHN 14:1-3

God is our refuge and strength,
a very present help in trouble.
Therefore we will not fear,
though the earth should change,
though the mountains shake in
the heart of the sea;
though its waters roar and foam,
though the mountains tremble
with its tumult.

PSALMS 46:1-3

Choices for the Service

PLANNING THE SERVICE

Memorial and funeral services are thanksgiving worship services to remember and honor the deceased. It is good and fitting for the services to reflect something of the uniqueness, the distinctive character and special qualities, of the person.

It is also important to keep in mind, as a contributor noted that "it is sometimes hard to remember that the service and arrangements are primarily for the benefit of the living. *What you are doing you are doing for the living.*" Another contributor added, "Think about and recall what you have liked and not liked about services you have attended. Let that help guide your choices."

Details for the worship services need to be completed. There are several things you may want to think about before the family meets with the pastor.

> *"The memory of the righteous*
> *is a blessing...."*
>
>
>
> PROVERBS 10:7A

BEGINNING WITH A "REMEMBERING CIRCLE"

What is a "Remembering Circle"? It is a gathering of family—sisters, brothers, in-laws, nieces, and nephews—assembled in a circle with the pastor for the purpose of reminiscing about the family member who has died, and to plan the funeral or memorial service.

In the words of some participants: "The 'Remembering Circle,' when the family gathered with the pastor to talk about Dad and things for the service, was especially meaningful to our family." "It was a time of both laughter and tears for us. It was a very special time!" "Someone said, 'All I've heard about are the bad things that happened. Then we started thinking about the good things, overcame the negative memories, and used the list of good things in the service.'"

One family member noted another important benefit, in some situations: "If the pastor did not know the person, some process is needed to help the pastor learn enough about the person to personalize the service."

The Remembering Circle helps all participants because:

- The family has a special time of remembering that will probably include both tears and laughter. This time of sharing nourishes the beginnings of healing from grief.

- Family members frequently discover from one another things—life stories—they had never known and would never know without sharing around the circle.

- Healing from the emotional injuries of a lifetime may begin if the sharing recalls the good things that happened.

- The pastor—even if he or she knows the person rather well—will get to know the person in a multi-dimensional way not otherwise possible.

If your pastor does not normally use the Remembering Circle, you may invite him or her to do so for your family.

When a Remembering Circle comes together, two things need to be done:

- First, the pastor says: *"Tell me about this person. I want to listen. I will be taking notes, but I will be listening carefully."*

- Second, the pastor asks *what the family wants in the service.* Together they decide:

1. What particular Scriptures, hymns, readings?
2. Who will participate? By doing what?
3. Other special requests?

This is the time to discuss:

• Do you choose to have a eulogy?

   If yes, who will give it? _____

• Will there be additional participants in the service?

   As Scripture readers? Who? _____

   _____

   As candlelighters? Who?_____

   _____

   Other service participants?
   (See also Music, next page.)

   Who?   Doing what?

   _____

   _____

   _____

   _____

   _____

MUSIC IN THE SERVICE

Hymns sung by the congregation. Hymn-singing is a traditional part of most services of worship. Congregational singing may be included in the services instead of or in addition to solos or other special music. "For us, singing of hymns provided a sense of community and support, a feeling of unity."

Ask musicians in your family. "We assumed our musician children would find it difficult and would not want to participate in their grandfather's service. Our pastor suggested that we allow them to decide. This was good advice.

"Our daughter is the church organist, and wanted to be organist for the service. Our son chose to sing.

"We're glad we checked it out and let them decide. They can say, 'I can't do that,' if they need to do so."

Instruments. A variety of musical instruments—as well as a variety of music—may be included if you choose to do so. "Music may be upbeat, celebrative, not mournful. The service can be a celebration of life. We used a guitar for music."

"Popular" music. "We chose to have the special music include a secular song that was an expression of the person's life. This was in addition to hymns and other special sacred music."

"We wanted the service to match him. We used some religious music and some down-to-earth popular music."

POSSIBLE MUSIC FOR THE SERVICE:

_____

_____

_____

_____

_____

_____

POSSIBLE MUSICIANS FOR THE SERVICE:

_____

_____

_____

_____

_____

OTHER SERVICE PARTICIPANTS

Other people besides the pastor and musicians may be included as participants in the service. "We invited several people to speak in addition to the pastor. We specifically asked some people ahead of time."

These are some options. You may think of several others.

- "[One or more] might share a story of their experience with the person being remembered."

- "There was also an opportunity for anyone else to say what they might like to say."

- An essay or poem that was a favorite of the deceased—or is a favorite of someone in the family—could be read by a family member or a friend.

- A friend or family member could read Scripture.

- A suitable composition written by the deceased could be read.

One contributor summed it up: "This was hard [emotionally], but nice."

Is there someone in the family—or among friends—
who might fittingly be included as a service participant?

Who?   Doing what?

_____

_____

_____

_____

_____

Have you not known?
Have you not heard?
The Lord is the everlasting God,
the Creator of the ends of the earth.
He does not faint or grow weary;
his understanding is unsearchable.
He gives power to the faint,
and strengthens the powerless.

Isaiah 40:28-29

THE EULOGY

Usually given by a family member or special friend, a eulogy, if used, is a reflection on the deceased person's life. It affirms the person's life—describes what was included in his or her life. In one instance, several family members were invited to write brief statements, which were all read by the person giving the eulogy.

"I gave the eulogy at my father's service. It was difficult but good to do. He had lived ninety-four years of his life somewhere else. People here did not know him. The church was full of my friends, so I told them about my father. Lots of people could not or would not do this, but it was good for me to do."

A PRINTED ORDER OF SERVICE

Ordinarily called a "bulletin," a printed order of worship not only includes guidance for the service. It may also contain other information such as:

- time and place of the committal service;
- memorial fund suggestion;
- time and place when the family will greet friends;
- funeral home arrangements;
- names of service participants, musicians, ushers, pallbearers, and guest book attendants.

With the capacity of contemporary copy machines, bulletin covers for memorial or funeral services may feature artwork by the deceased or something specially prepared for this purpose by a friend or family member.

"For us, a printed order of service provided a sense of order and a secure feeling."

"We had a printed order of service. It was more like a regular church service."

WHAT TO INCLUDE IN THE ORDER OF SERVICE:

_____

_____

_____

_____

_____

I will call to mind the deeds of the Lord;
I will remember your wonders of old.

PSALM 77:11

OTHER RITES

If other rites and ceremonies are to be observed, your pastor will need to know what they are in order to coordinate with the other leaders and place them in faithful relationship to the services of the church.

Will there be military ceremonies?

Yes _____ No _____

An honor guard, a color guard?

Yes _____ No _____

A gun salute?

Yes _____ No _____

A flag presentation?

Yes _____ No _____

Masonic ceremonies?

Yes _____ No _____

Eastern Star rituals?

Yes _____ No _____

Other lodge rites?

Yes _____ No _____

If yes, who needs to be contacted?

_____

_____

_____

PARTICIPATION OF CHILDREN

Loss by death wounds deeply. The emotional impact compares to the physical blow and shock of major surgery. Children feel this hurt intensely. Especially if the surviving family includes younger children—or g. andchildren—give careful thought to ways of including the children.

Children may be invited to *bring or make something to put in the grave.* Children sometimes bring drawings they have made, flowers, or other appropriate items to leave in a grave.

School-age children may be asked what they might like to do, even in the service. Seek their ideas! For example, perhaps a child or a grandchild, a niece or a nephew, would like to serve as a candlelighter at a funeral or memorial service. Depending on their ages, children may hand out bulletins, serve as guest book attendants, or help greet and entertain out-of-town guests. Do not underestimate the potential of children from the second grade upwards. Talk to the children. See if they have ideas. Children often surprise us.

Are there children to be included?

Yes _____   No _____

Names   Possible contributions

_____

_____

_____

SEATING—FAMILY AND SPECIAL GROUPS

Family seating. Since a funeral or memorial service is a time of worship, it is appropriate for the family to sit as part of the worshiping congregation. Most often, the family sits at the front of the church near the pulpit. However, a family may sit in varying parts of the church depending on family needs and wishes.

"We sat in a different part of the church from where the family normally sits."

"Be aware of where the family sits, especially if anyone has allergies. In choosing a place for them to be seated, be sure to consider the location of flowers."

Seating for other special groups. Will reserved seating be needed for special groups? What groups may wish to have reserved sections?

_____

_____

_____

*God is spirit, and those who worship him
must worship in spirit and truth.*

JOHN 4:24

SPECIAL REQUESTS FOR SCRIPTURE
OR OTHER READINGS

Are there specific Scriptures—favorites of either the deceased or family members—which you want the pastor to include in the service?

Scriptures:

_____

_____

Other readings:

_____

_____

It is good to give thanks to the Lord,
to sing praises to your name, O Most High;
to declare your steadfast love in the morning,
and your faithfulness by night,
to the music of the lute and the harp,
to the melody of the lyre.

PSALM 92:1-3

AUDIO- OR VIDEOTAPING

When technically possible, the service may be audio- or video-recorded. Recordings create the possibility of hearing later something missed because of the emotion of the moment and of reliving something which was especially meaningful and helpful.

Do you want to make audiotapes or videotapes of the service?

Yes _____ No _____

If so, who could be asked to oversee the project?

_____

_____

THE CASKET IN THE FUNERAL SERVICE

Before the funeral is the appropriate time for the casket to be open, to give friends and family a chance to say their final "good-byes." Just before the funeral service begins, it is fitting for the casket to be closed. The funeral service changes the focus from the physical body to, in the words of St. Paul, the "spiritual body." When worship begins, God is foremost. Closing the casket begins the turn of our attention from death to faith in the resurrection and new life.

In a church which has a Lord's Table or altar at the front, an appropriate placement for the casket is at right angles to the Lord's Table, not sideways. The head of the coffin may be turned toward the congregation— unless the deceased was ordained, in which event the head is put toward the Lord's Table. This suggests the position of laity sitting in the pews and pastors in the chancel. Some traditions choose other arrangements for location of the casket.

Whenever the arrangement of the church and the physical strength of the pallbearers permit, it is fitting, as a sign of respect, for the casket to be physically carried by the pallbearers rather than being rolled in and out on wheels. In any case, placement of the coffin should insure that it is not the center of worship.

As an expression of honor, the casket often is brought into the church last, after the family has entered and immediately before the service begins. Likewise, as a sign of respect, the casket may be taken out first, fol- lowed immediately by the family. In both cases, it is cus- tomary for the pastor to precede the casket.

As plans are made, it is important to remember that a funeral or memorial service is Christian worship. Christ holds the service. Christ is the host. Those worshiping are guests.

A PALL

Some traditions use a pall, which is a cloth used to cover or drape the casket. In the case of military veterans, the national flag often is draped as a pall over the casket.

Increasingly, a Christian flag is used as a pall. Often provided by a church, the Christian flag may be used over and over for funeral services. A pall symbolizes the deceased's service in the faith and—by covering the casket—symbolizes the equality of everyone before God.

CARS AND DRIVERS

You may choose to use personal vehicles, funeral cars provided by the funeral directors, or both to transport members of the immediate family to the graveside service. In either case, you will need to specify riders and may need to designate drivers.

For the services, who will drive? Which cars? Who will ride in each car?

1. Car: _____

   Driver: _____

   Riders: _____

   _____

2. Car: _____

    Driver: _____

    Riders: _____

    _____

3. Car: _____

    Driver: _____

    Riders: _____

    _____

4. Car: _____

    Driver: _____

    Riders: _____

    _____

Who can notify these people for you?

_____

_____

_____

CHECKLIST

Consider:

☐ BEGINNING WITH A "REMEMBERING CIRCLE" (pages 106-108)

☐ MUSIC IN THE SERVICE (pages 109-110)

☐ OTHER SERVICE PARTICIPANTS (pages 111-112)

☐ THE EULOGY (page 113)

☐ A PRINTED ORDER OF SERVICE (pages 113-114)

☐ OTHER RITES (page 115)

☐ PARTICIPATION OF CHILDREN (page 116)

☐ SEATING—FAMILY AND SPECIAL GROUPS (page 117)

☐ SPECIAL REQUESTS FOR SCRIPTURE, OTHER READINGS (page 118)

☐ AUDIO- OR VIDEOTAPING (page 119)

☐ THE PLACEMENT OF THE CASKET (pages 119-120)

☐ THE USE OF A PALL (page 121)

☐ CARS—WHICH ONES, DRIVERS, RIDERS (pages 121-122)

I cry aloud to God,
 aloud to God, that he may hear me.
In the day of my trouble I seek the Lord;
 in the night my hand is stretched out
  without wearying;
 my soul refuses to be comforted.
You keep my eyelids from closing:
 I am so troubled that I cannot speak.
I commune with my heart in the night;
 I meditate and search my spirit:
"Will the Lord spurn forever,
 and never again be favorable?
Has his steadfast love ceased forever?"

PSALM 77:1-2, 4, 6-8A

Getting Help Afterward

OTHERS WANT TO TELL YOU...

"It was helpful for me to be told that the grieving process can take three or four years. I expected to lay it aside in six months."

"Try to talk with people who have been through it. Friends listen, but people who have been through it may be particularly helpful."

"Do not be afraid to ask for help. You may be positively surprised at the response. Ask your spouse, a friend, your pastor."

"Don't be surprised if—almost immediately—you begin recalling and to some degree reliving previous significant deaths and grief experiences of your life."

"Death 'replays' earlier deaths. I re-experienced my father's death through all of this."

"Anger is a normal feeling in grief. Don't be surprised by it."

"Try to be tolerant of varied responses from other people—both in their words and their behavior. They may say things that seem offensive to you, causing you to think, 'Why would they say something like that?' It may be that they don't know what to say and say things that may be inappropriate."

WHAT TO EXPECT...

The following summary of what to expect during the grieving process is brief, accurate, and essentially complete. It is summarized from Ernest Morgan's book *Dealing Creatively with Death*.[13]

Denial, shock, numbness—protecting us from realization of the magnitude of the loss, especially in the case of sudden loss.

Emotional release—often in a flood of tears, realization of loss, beginning of healing.

Depression, loneliness, isolation.

Physical symptoms, physical sensations—emptiness or hole in the pit of the stomach; lump in the throat; tightness in chest; sighing; tiring or weakness of body; lack of energy; dry mouth; headaches; etc. A wide variety of minor or serious digestive, respiratory, hormonal, cardiovascular, and immune system deficiency symptoms are possible.

Panic—when a person feels unable to cope with an unknown future or feels that there is something wrong with her or him.

Remorse—ranging from the almost universal sense of one's shortcomings to the intense guilt often experienced on the loss of a child, or when there are unresolved conflicts, or in the case of suicide.

Anger—at the deceased for dying, or at anyone who might be blamed for the death, or at God. Also anger at self, and guilt—for all the things I should have done or said, or all the things I wish I hadn't done or said. This is normal, but may be difficult to face and share.

Need to talk—to express feelings, share memories, find meaning in the person's life.

Taking positive actions in response to death—like working to avoid similar deaths for others, reaching out to persons similarly bereaved, completing projects of, or on behalf of, the deceased. This is always healing, but especially helpful for relief of guilt.

Readjustment—reaching out in new relationships and experiences.

SUPPORT GROUPS CONTACTS

First, in your local community, check with these agencies for information about existing programs and groups in your area:

- Hospices
- Public mental health agencies
- Private mental health agencies
- Hospitals
- Churches
- Church-related organizations

Hear my prayer, O Lord;
let my cry come to you.
Do not hide your face from me
in the day of my distress.
Incline your ear to me;
answer me speedily in the day
when I call.

PSALM 102:1-2

If you are unsuccessful in locating a group locally, contact one of the following national organizations for information about groups and programs nearest where you live.

FOR SUPPORT IF YOU HAVE LOST A CHILD:

Compassionate Friends
P.O. Box 3696
Oak Brook, IL 60522
Telephone: (708) 990-0010

Parents of Murdered Children
100 East 8th, B41
Cincinnati, OH 45202
Telephone: (513) 721-5683

or in Canada:
Bereaved Families of Ontario
214 Merton Street, Suite 204
Toronto, Ont. M4S 1A6
Telephone: (416) 440-0290

FOR SUPPORT WHEN YOU ARE WIDOWED:

THEOS
322 Blvd of the Allies
Pittsburgh, PA 15222
Telephone: (412) 471-7779

For support after a suicide loss:

Survivors Helping Survivors
Emergency Department
St. Luke's Hospital
2900 W. Oklahoma Avenue
Milwaukee, WI 53215
Telephone: (414) 649-6000

See, the home of God is among mortals.
He will dwell with them as their God;
they will be his peoples,
and God himself will be with them;
he will wipe every tear from their eyes.

Revelation 21:3-4a

For the Lord is good;
his steadfast love endures
forever, and his faithfulness
to all generations.

PSALM 100:5

Notes

1. "Memorial Societies are cooperative, nonprofit consumer organizations, democratically run, that help their members get simplicity, dignity, and economy in funeral arrangements through advance planning. They are not run by funeral directors." Ernest and Jenifer Morgan, *Dealing Creatively with Death: A Manual of Death Education and Simple Burial,* 12th ed. (Bayside, N.Y.: Barclay, 1990), 67. See also pages 68-70, 119-25.

   For information contact: *Continental Association of Funeral and Memorial Societies* (CAFMS), 7910 Woodmont Ave., Suite 1430, Bethesda, MD 20814. Telephone (301) 913-0030.

2. "Private option" is a nonprofessional funeral. "Some groups and individuals care for their own dead without the assistance of a funeral director. A few are religious groups. Others are rural families" (Morgan, 59).

   For information see: Lisa Carlson, *Caring for Your Own Dead* (Hinesburg, Vt.: Upper Access, 1987).

3. Carlson, 36, 340.
4. Carlson, 316.
5. Carlson, 314-15.
6. Carlson, 38.
7. Carlson, 38.
8. Carlson, 317.
9. Morgan, 58.
10. Morgan, 57.
11. Carlson, 24-31.
12. Morgan, 57.
13. Morgan, 22.

Reference Reading

Carlson, Lisa. *Caring for Your Own Dead.* Hinesburg, Vt.: Upper Access, 1987.

Kinnaman, Gary. *My Companion through Grief.* Ann Arbor: Servant, 1996.

Mitsch, Raymond R. *Grieving the Loss of Someone You Love.* Ann Arbor: Servant, 1993.

Morgan, Ernest and Jenifer. *Dealing Creatively with Death: A Manual of Death Education and Simple Burial.* Bayside, N.Y.: Barclay, 1990.

Packer, J.I. *A Grief Sanctified.* Ann Arbor: Servant, 1996.

Parachin, Victor M. *Grief Relief.* St. Louis: CBP Press, 1991.

Wolterstorff, Nicolas. *Lament for a Son.* Grand Rapids, Mich.: Eerdmans, 1987.

Westberg, Granger E. *Good Grief.* Minneapolis: Augsburg-Fortress, 1971.

"To Do Later" List

Priority Number		Completed
☐	Write thank you notes.	☐
☐	See an attorney. What needs to be done?	☐
	______________________________	
☐	Change insurance policies.	
	Home ______________________	☐
	Car ______________________	☐
	______________________________	☐
	______________________________	☐
☐	Living will may need to be updated.	☐
☐	Keep careful records for income tax purposes.	☐
☐	Notify the post office of any necessary address changes.	☐
☐	______________________________	☐
	______________________________	
☐	______________________________	☐
	______________________________	

PRIORITY

NUMBER   COMPLETED

☐ _____ ☐

☐ _____ ☐

☐ _____ ☐

☐ _____ ☐

☐ _____ ☐

☐ _____ ☐

☐ _____ ☐

☐ _____ ☐

☐ _____ ☐

APPOINTMENTS

DAY OF DEATH

TODAY is:

Day of the week _____

Date _____

Time _____   Pastor at your home

Time _____   Funeral director at your home

Time _____

      Who? _____

      Where? _____

Time _____

      Who? _____

      Where? _____

Time _____

      Who? _____

      Where? _____

Time _____

      Who? _____

      Where? _____

Time _____

      Who? _____

      Where? _____

APPOINTMENTS

DAY AFTER THE DEATH

TODAY is:

Day of the week _____

Date _____

Time _____   Funeral Director at funeral home

Time _____   Cemetery?

Time _____   Bank?

Time _____   Florist?

Time _____

        Who? _____

        Where? _____

Time _____

        Who? _____

        Where? _____

Time _____

        Who? _____

        Where? _____

Time _____

        Who? _____

        Where? _____

APPOINTMENTS

DAY BEFORE THE MEMORIAL OR FUNERAL SERVICE

TODAY is:

Day of the week _____

Date _____

Time _____ Pastor at the church

Time _____ Family viewing at the funeral home

Time _____ Public viewing at the funeral home

Time _____

      Who? _____

      Where? _____

Time _____

      Who? _____

      Where? _____

Time _____

      Who? _____

      Where? _____

Time _____

      Who? _____

      Where? _____

APPOINTMENTS

DAY OF THE MEMORIAL OR FUNERAL SERVICE

TODAY is:

Day of the week _____

Date _____

Time _____   Memorial or funeral service

Time _____   Committal service

(graveside service, unless scheduled for a different day)

Time _____   Leave for service

Time _____   View flowers

Time _____   Funeral dinner

Time _____

Who? _____

Where? _____

Time _____

Who? _____

Where? _____

Time _____

Who? _____

Where? _____

BLANK PAGES FOR NOTES

BLANK PAGES FOR NOTES

_____

_____

_____

_____

_____

_____

_____

_____

_____

_____

_____

_____

_____

_____

_____

_____

_____

_____

_____

BLANK PAGES FOR NOTES

BLANK PAGES FOR NOTES

BLANK PAGES FOR NOTES

BLANK PAGES FOR NOTES

_____

_____

_____

_____

_____

_____

_____

_____

_____

_____

_____

_____

_____

_____

_____

_____

_____

_____

BLANK PAGES FOR NOTES

BLANK PAGES FOR NOTES

BLANK PAGES FOR NOTES

BLANK PAGES FOR NOTES

_____

_____

_____

_____

_____

_____

_____

_____

_____

_____

_____

_____

_____

_____

_____

_____

_____

_____

_____

BLANK PAGES FOR NOTES

Another Book of Interest from Vine Books

Grieving the Loss of Someone You Love
Daily Meditations to Help You through the Grieving Process

RAYMOND R. MITSCH AND LYNN BROOKSIDE

Few losses are as painful as the death of someone close. No valley is as vast as grief, no journey as personal and life-challenging. The seventy thoughtful reflections in this book will strengthen and encourage you, and will help you to sort through the many emotions you must face during this time of loss. **$9.99 compact**

Available at your Christian bookstore or from
Servant Publications • Dept. 209 • PO Box 7455
Ann Arbor, Michigan 48107
Please include payment plus $2.75 per book
for postage and handling.
Send for our free catalog.